CONTENTS

INTRODUCTION

THE IMAGE OF A GYPSY as a carefree, swarthy, dark-haired nomad wandering aimlessly round the country in a brightly painted caravan has been perpetuated by generations of artists and writers who have chosen to portray romantic fiction rather than the often stark reality. Unfortunately, this colourful image has become a yardstick by which the authenticity of the 'true' Gypsy continues to be measured. It is commonly believed that the real Gypsy disappeared along with the horse-drawn living wagon, a belief partly based on the occurrence of fair skin and blue eyes amongst the Travellers of modern times. But 'out' marriages with the settled population account for the eye colour and, as they did for milkmen and other tradesmen, motor vehicles displaced horse-drawn wagons as the preferred mode of travel: the wagon had served its purpose for the time, as had the donkey and cart before that. Gypsies have been part of British history for over five hundred years and have remained apart from other travelling groups that have appeared over the years. The similarities in lifestyle and occupations of the different groups have blurred the distinction for the casual observer, resulting in a misconception that all Travellers are Gypsies. They are not, and similarly not all Gypsies are Travellers.

In Britain Gypsies and Scottish Travellers are recognised ethnic minorities, each of them having their own traditions and culture, the origins of which stretch back for centuries. Their relationship with the settled community has not always been an easy one. From the outset, Gypsies have been regarded with suspicion. A propensity for fortune-telling created an air of mystery and, when not engaged in work or trade, they also kept their distance, travelling light in order to make a swift departure.

The apparent ease with which they disappeared – here today, gone tomorrow – perhaps explains why they were sometimes described as 'the secret people', and yet they have contributed to all areas of British life: as service providers, bringers of news, entertainers, preachers, and in military and war service.

Opposite:
A cupboard door inside the Durham *vardo* exhibited at Ryedale Folk Museum. It is painted freehand in yellow, crimson and grass green, colours that are popular in wagon decoration.

TRAVELLING GROUPS IN BRITAIN

IT COULD EASILY be supposed that, before the invention of the bicycle, our ancestors barely moved outside their own parish boundaries, unless they were fortunate enough to own a horse and cart on which to travel into the nearest town or to an adjacent village. It may be true that generations of some families remained within a 10-mile radius of their birthplace but, out of necessity, others were forced to travel much further afield to seek employment. Many travelled as a way of life, following the traditions of their forefathers and remaining separate from, but to some degree dependent upon, the settled communities through which they passed.

For a variety of reasons, Britain has always had an itinerant population. In Tudor times poverty was widespread and, driven by the need to survive, labourers travelled in search of work, particularly when harvests were poor. Soldiers, on their return from fighting overseas, were left at the coast to find their own way back to their homes, begging on their way for food to survive, and pedlars and petty chapmen criss-crossed the country with their wares. Swelling their numbers were the dispossessed, domestic servants who had been dismissed, the militia, and artisans following essential trades such as thatching and masonry.

Before the advent of living wagons – or caravans – travel was by horse and cart or on foot. An original print published by Pyne & Nattes in 1807.

By the fourteenth century a large network of fairs had been established across the country by royal charter. These drew people from far and wide and, although initially for trading, they later attracted those who provided entertainment, including travelling musicians, strolling players, clowns and acrobats, all of whom saw an opportunity to part the visitors from their money. Sideshows and booths offering the spectacle of human and animal curiosities came later. Britain's modern travelling fairs and circuses can trace some of their origins back to those times.

A substantial network of canals had grown up by the early nineteenth century. Crews to man the boats were recruited from those who had once worked as labourers. For these boatmen, the movement of cargo in an increasingly competitive market necessitated many days spent away from home. Whole families began living and working on the boats, with children being born along the way. Over time a distinct community evolved. They developed their own style of dress and began to paint their narrowboats with bright motifs and pictures. It was perhaps because of this similarity with the painted wagons of the Romanies that the two groups were thought to be connected, with the canal folk becoming wrongly identified as 'water Gypsies'.

The Romanies – or Gypsies – are not indigenous to Britain. When they first appeared in Britain, they were believed to be Egyptians, the word becoming shortened to 'Gyptian', and then eventually to 'Gypsy', the term now erroneously applied to almost anyone following an itinerant lifestyle. Since then, there has been much speculation as to their true origins, but their language – Romani or Romanes, which is a form of Sanskrit – suggests that the Gypsies of Europe have their origins in north-west India, the first groups having left there over one thousand years ago. Some, it is believed, were driven out by invading Turks and Arabs, or taken as slaves to Persia, while others left of their own free will in search of work.

A fair day in the 1830s. Fairs were an important part of Gypsy life, providing opportunities for trade and a meeting place for family members.

7

An encampment of Gypsies in Europe. Gypsies in Britain would have been of similar appearance. From an old print of a 1604 engraving by Jacques Callot.

There appears to have been no mass exodus from India; rather, they departed in groups over a period of time. Inevitably, words were picked up from whichever country they spent time in, and from these it has been possible to work out the probable routes taken during their travels, and the length of time spent in each country visited.

The exact date of the first group's arrival in Britain is not known. An early reference appeared in the accounts of the Lord High Treasurer of Scotland in 1492, recording a payment of 4s being made to a Peter Ker, and mentioning 'the King of the Romais'. Just a few days later, a payment was made to the messenger of 'the King of the Rowmais'. This was followed by a 1505 entry recording the payment of ten French crowns to a party of 'Egiptianis'. In England, in 1514, one of the witnesses at the inquest into the death of Richard Hunne, a merchant tailor accused of heresy and subsequently found hanged in his cell, was an 'Egypcyan' woman 'who could tell marvellous things simply by looking into a person's hand'.

Around the coast, at a time when overseas trade brought foreign ships into British seaports, it is unlikely that Romanies would have particularly stood out amongst the exotically dressed merchants from the Mediterranean, but for many they were unlike any other group of people they had previously seen. They were dark-skinned, spoke an odd language and wore strange clothes. That they claimed to be refugees from religious persecution may at first have elicited some sympathy, and doubtless their skill as entertainers and musicians made them welcome visitors. By the late 1520s attitudes had changed. Gypsies were arriving in increased numbers, and an Act of 1530, referring to 'dyverse and many outlandysshe people calling themselfes

Egyptians', banned further immigration and required those already in England to leave voluntarily or be deported.

They originally had their own surnames but eventually borrowed new ones from the host society, some of them coming from the people in the locality where they happened to be stopping. Others took them from the great land-owning families, such as Hearn, Gray, Stanley and Buckland, possibly in the hope that it would afford them some protection against increasing hostility and the legislation being passed against them. Marriage with locals also brought new names into the community and eventually their original names disappeared.

Although the Romanies may be described as the first immigrants of wandering habit, in Scotland nomadic people have a long history going back to at least the twelfth century, being descended in part from tinsmiths who travelled for work, forging not just pots and pans for domestic use, but also the weapons and shields so necessary in battle. Adding to their number were those who were forced from their homes during the famine of 1623. Some Scottish Travellers have well-known clan names, which suggests that also among their ancestors were refugees from the Battle of Culloden of 1745. The Highland Clearances also rendered many families homeless, and unsympathetic landowners turned many off their crofts during the 1840s potato famine, increasing their numbers yet again.

These people are believed to be Scottish Travellers. The covering on the cart resembles a bender tent.

The dialects used by Scottish Travellers contain old Gaelic, indicative of lines of descent from the ancient Scots, and some words from Irish Traveller dialect. Many more are from the Romani language, a result of intermarriage with the immigrant Romanies who criss-crossed the border with England.

Often referred to as 'Tinkers', a name taken from their past occupation of metalworking and deemed pejorative by Scottish Travellers, those groups from the Highlands identify themselves as Travellers, while those from the Lowland and Border areas regard themselves as Gypsies. Both sometimes identify themselves as Nawkens, which translates as 'no home'.

Irish Travellers, or Pavee, have been coming to mainland Britain from at least the 1850s. Families following the trade of 'tinker' were living in tents at the time of the 1851 census, although individual Travellers from Ireland were noted in parish registers in the eighteenth century. Some believe that they are the descendants of those who were evicted from their land by Cromwell but their language suggests they are descended in part from an

Irish Travellers were not indigenous to Britain but appeared in small groups at least as early as the 1840s. *Illustrated London News*, May 1845.

Scottish Travellers on the road.

ethnic group that pre-dates the arrival of the Celts into Ireland. Though there is a probability of the Irish Travellers intermarrying with refugees of the Irish potato famine, strong cultural traditions and beliefs continue to set them apart from the settled population. Despite similarities in lifestyle and occupations, and occasional marriage with Romany or Scottish Travellers, there is little to suggest a common ancestry links them.

New Travellers, known as New Age Travellers when they started to form in the 1970s, are members of the settled community who for social, economic or environmental reasons moved into old buses and lorries and took to the road. Although not Gypsies, they are fast becoming 'traditional' in that, in some cases, a third generation has been born to the lifestyle.

The different terms used to describe Britain's Gypsies can cause some confusion. To be a Gypsy carried harsh penalties during certain periods in history. It could also be problematic when seeking employment. Increasingly, as a self-ascription, the term most favoured by Gypsies themselves was 'Traveller' and it continues to be used, even by the second and third generations of settled Gypsies who have never followed a travelling lifestyle. However, since 'Traveller' has become a catch-all for almost anyone of nomadic habit in Britain, 'Gypsy' is once again a preferred choice, along with 'Romany'.

Historically, the traditional travelling groups of Britain are the Scottish Travellers and the Romanies.

Scottish Travellers at Pitlochry.

TRAVELLING PATTERNS AND ABODES

TRAVELLING was a way of life for most Gypsies not simply because it was a long-held tradition, but because they had to feed and clothe themselves. Legislation over the centuries had an impact on their travelling patterns. Soon after the 1530 Act, another was passed for 'the punishment of vagrants, those practising the "crafty sciences" and people feigning knowledge in palmistry'. Punishment was severe for those who were caught and included the pillory, whipping or the severing of an ear.

In 1547 an Act was directed at wandering persons and those not seeking work. Punishments now included enslavement and branding, encouragement enough to keep their sojourns in each parish as brief as possible. Following this, in 1551-2, an Act against 'Tynkers and Pedlars' forbade them to travel about without licence from the justices. Two years later, 'Egyptians' were forbidden to enter England and anyone caught bringing them in was liable to a fine of 40s. Those who did enter and were still there forty days later could be sentenced to death: thirteen were hanged at the Suffolk assizes just for being Gypsies.

In 1562, however, it was declared that Gypsies born in England could not be deported. By the very early seventeenth century, Gypsies were having their children baptised in parishes as widespread as Devon and Suffolk.

Nonetheless, Acts continued to be passed that made travelling as a way of life very challenging. In 1597 all wandering tinkers and those pretending to be Egyptians were declared rogues and vagabonds, and a similar Act in 1743 covered Gypsies and Egyptians pretending to tell fortunes. In 1822 the Turnpike Roads Act made any Gypsy camping on the side of a turnpike road liable to a fine, and this was quickly followed by the Vagrancy Act, which made it illegal for anyone to sleep out in the open in a tent or cart. Even allowing a horse to stray or building a fire too close to the highway could result in a spell in prison. One way of avoiding the law was to stop at a place close to a parish or county boundary, so that it would be possible to strike camp quickly and cross the border into the relative safety of a neighbouring jurisdiction.

Opposite: Wagon interiors were often as decorative as the exteriors. The amount of bevelled glass and gold leaf used depended on the wealth of the owner.

Bender tent, c. 1915. Benders were in common use by Gypsies and Scottish Travellers until well into the twentieth century, and some families continued to use them as late as the 1970s.

Until tents came into regular use during the eighteenth century, Gypsies found shelter in barns and outhouses or stopped in lodgings. Bender tents were easily erected and taken down, thus enabling a hasty departure from any neighbourhood where their liberty may have been threatened or if there was a promise of work in another area. They were made from rods of bent hazel, one end of which was inserted into the ground and the other into holes in a ridge pole, and were covered in whatever fabric was available, from army serge to hessian sacks acquired from farms. The simple shelter could be easily transported by donkey or handcart and provided immediate cover at the next chosen spot.

A less usual version, seen at Finchley Common in 1818, was a tent-shaped construction formed from boughs of trees that were then covered with turf. In the latter half of the nineteenth century, some Gypsies replaced their improvised tents with ready-made ex-army bell tents. The tent-dwelling Gypsies kept their possessions to a minimum. Small items such as plates, cutlery and cooking utensils were easily portable by handcart or donkey, but furniture was not. Ferns, bracken or straw could form a bed; a fallen log or upturned bucket could provide seating, and a minimum of clothes could be packed away in a single box.

The Gypsy caravan – or *vardo* in Romani – did not appear in Britain until at least the mid-nineteenth century, its forerunner being little more than a bender tent erected on a flat cart. At an overnight stop, the bender could

easily be lifted from the cart and placed on a convenient flat piece of ground. Initially, the purpose-built living wagons were of basic design and bore little resemblance to the brightly coloured, richly carved wagons that some equate with the 'real' Romany. Although the occupiers sometimes built their own vans, by the 1870s country wheelwrights were being commissioned to make them. As time passed, they evolved into those that have come to be identified as the Gypsy caravan, including the 'Reading', the 'Ledge', the 'Burton' and the 'Bowtop'. The most impressive – and expensive – were beautifully painted and highlighted in gold leaf. This extravagance was carried through

A Yorkshire open-lot *vardo*, so-called because there are no doors at the front. It was used in the York area by the Smith family. Now at Ryedale Folk Museum in North Yorkshire.

15

Tent-shaped
structures fitting
the description
of those seen on
Finchley Common
in 1818.

to the interiors, with etched, bevelled glass and painted ceilings. During the restoration of one old Reading, what was thought to be the original linoleum was uncovered. The Victoria and Albert Museum later confirmed it to be a very rare example of hand-painted oilcloth, the type used for old sailing ships. Most wagons, however, were fairly plain. In 1904, a simply built and decorated Reading made by Dunton & Sons of Reading cost approximately £70. The wealthier the customer, the more ornate the carving and elaborate the decoration, although in times of hardship there was little sentiment when it came to selling them on.

The bow- or barrel-top was popular in the north of the country but elsewhere the Reading was the type most favoured. A vehicle was required that was suitable for pulling off on to rough ground or crossing fords, and the tall wheels of the Reading, between which the straight-sided, high-arched body was slung, met these needs better than vehicles with wheels situated beneath the body. Gypsies travelled to Reading from all over to have their wagons built, but although named after the town, the Reading type was also built by other wheelwrights, including Wicks of Wisbech, F. J. Thomas of Chertsey, Williams of Leighton Buzzard and D. Macintosh of London.

Members of the Allum family travelling with their wagon in Cambridge in 1932.

As with most other wagon types, a stove was situated to the left of the entrance, which was at the shaft end, thus ensuring that, when travelling along the road, the chimney missed the overhang of trees. A rack at the back carried various domestic articles, and underneath the wagon, at the back, was a cupboard for storing food. With a double bed built along the wall opposite the door, and a shorter bed beneath to accommodate the children, it was a compact home on wheels. Nonetheless, some wagon-owning families continued to sleep beneath the wagon or in a tent, and meals were more often than not cooked over an outside fire.

For some families, observing strict cleanliness rituals was important. Separate birthing tents for expectant mothers were set at some distance from the living wagon. A month after the child's birth, the tent was burned along with the bedding, and anything else associated with the tent was also destroyed. Living wagons were too valuable to be used thus, and so contamination was to be avoided at all costs. The burning of the wagon on the death of the owner was a tradition observed by many, but by no means all, particularly if the death had occurred elsewhere.

Depending on the occupations followed, the wagon served more than one purpose. In 1869 a Sussex parish report stated that 'On Ashdown Forest reside numbers of those strange people [who] come down to the villages and towns in houses on wheels or those large vans which comprise dwelling-house, shop and vehicle in one ...'

Although by necessity dependent on the settled society as customers for their services, Gypsies also relied on them for seasonal paid work. Travelling patterns were therefore partly defined by the agricultural calendar and the dates of fairs, race meetings and markets. Family traditions also had an influence, in that consecutive generations were likely to follow the same circuit as their forefathers.

From springtime onwards, visits were made to fairs and markets to replenish or sell on stock. Wanstead Flats was known as the 'Gypsy Fair' because so many Gypsies made it the first stop in their travelling season. Race meetings were included in the itinerary for both work and pleasure. One family could regularly be seen at the races at Ascot, Molesey, Epsom and Brighton, and even frequented the Cambridge and Oxford Boat Race and Henley Regatta. Wherever there was a potential customer, there was an opportunity to do a deal.

Those with established routes made return visits to familiar villages and farms, some undertaking long-distance travel, others remaining largely within one county. It was seldom that Gypsies travelled continuously. For some the travelling year began with the potato planting and ended with pea

An open-lot *vardo* originally built c. 1910 and used in County Durham; now located at the Ryedale Folk Museum.

picking, but for others the last port of call was the hop gardens at hopping time, an annual pilgrimage made by large numbers of families. As with the fairs, it provided an opportunity to meet with those they had not seen for many months, and for the young to meet potential spouses under the watchful eyes of their parents. New babies were shown off and perhaps baptised by an itinerant missionary or local vicar, and couples married. When the harvest finished, the travelling hop-pickers made their way to the urban areas.

In the nineteenth century, with the coming of the railways and other improved transport links, towns and villages grew, drawing in the people from the countryside in search of better prospects and lifestyles. This in turn presented a work opportunity for travelling dealers and traders, and many began to spend winters on the outskirts of towns and cities, maybe camping on a convenient area of heath or even a derelict patch of land within the town itself. An added benefit of stopping on heathland close to a town was the abundant availability of natural materials from which Gypsies could make items to sell, as well as easy access to potential customers. If they were fortunate, they found land that could be taken on a long-term lease, thereby attaining a degree of security.

A Gypsy encampment on Putney Common. Putney attracted many Gypsies during the winter months. From *The Graphic*, June 1870.

In time, when the elderly and the sick were unable to take to the roads again, they stayed behind. The youngest family members were left in their care and, gradually, winter quarters became permanent stopping places. By the mid-nineteenth century, places where these so-called 'Gypsyeries' could be found included Blackpool, Blackpatch in Birmingham, Bournemouth, Tadley in Hampshire, and around the Notting Hill potteries in London. In Kent, a very large encampment began to grow on the Belvedere Marsh, and in Sussex there was one at Jarvis Brook. The 1881 census for Putney and Mitcham, in particular, recorded large numbers of tent and van dwellers. Ruislip Common was another favoured stopping place, as were Wimbledon Common, Battersea and Wandsworth.

Earlier still, Gypsies had become firmly established in the New Forest, Hampshire, many travelling away only to undertake seasonal work within the same county. A few families travelled further afield, sometimes as far as the Midlands, but they returned to spend the winters in the forest. In about 1830, the Reverend James Crabb, a reforming minister who did much work among the Gypsies, put the numbers residing in the forest and Southampton at several hundred.

Before the enclosure movement, Norwood in Surrey was a principal stopping place of the so-called 'London-side' Gypsies, but during the late eighteenth and early nineteenth centuries they were subjected to a series of police raids, which resulted in the whole group being put in prison as vagrants. They eventually moved further northwards and the area in Norwood where they had regularly stopped became known as Gipsy Hill.

A Reading wagon with bender tents providing additional accommodation.

The caves at Wick, in the north of Scotland, where a Scottish Traveller family lived.

At Kirk Yetholm in the Scottish Borders the Gypsies founded their own 'kingdom', even going as far as establishing a 'royal palace' in a cottage on Tinklers Row and crowning their own 'king' or 'queen'. They lived there according to their own customs but travelled out in the spring. Further north, the caves at Wick were the home for one group of Scottish Travellers.

In Wales, a colony became firmly established by the Welsh lakes, the founding father of which was Abram Wood, who had travelled from the West Country during the mid-eighteenth century.

As an alternative to choosing a winter stopping place on the edge of an urban area, rented property was sought in towns. In some cases, rent was paid for the full twelve months to ensure a safe haven to return to when the travelling season finished, or, alternatively, rooms were taken in cheap lodging houses. Others had relations already in permanent residence in their chosen town, on whose property they could pull up their vans or put up their tents. Railway arches were another choice, and sympathetic innkeepers and stable owners allowed them to use their yards. In 1891, in Battersea, there was a total of twenty-eight families spread between Mills Yard, Wheeler's Yard, Gurling Yard and Donovan's Yard. In addition to these, there were wagons stopping along Battersea Park Road and Victoria Road.

For these seasonal travellers, their sojourn within or close to a town continued until the advent of spring, when they would again take to the road to seek work in the fields or head for the first fair of the season, and so the travelling year once again began its familiar cycle.

The crowning of the 'Queen' at Kirk Yetholm, Scottish Borders.

EARNING A LIVING

THE MAIN DRIVING FORCE behind the search for work was the same for any sector of the working population, be it settled or travelling; like villagers and townsfolk, Gypsies had to provide for their families.

For many, the horse fairs were an important source of income. Throughout the nineteenth century transport was still dependent upon horse power, whether bus, tram, cab or coach. Ambulances and other emergency vehicles had yet to be mechanised, and fields were still ploughed by heavy horses. Ever ready for the opportunity to do a deal, some Gypsies kept a long train of horses that they drove from village to village en route to the next fair in their schedule.

While fairs and markets were necessary places for selling and replenishing stock, they also provided an opportunity to branch out into other areas of trade. Gingerbread stalls became a regular feature, and some Gypsies set up coconut shies and 'Aunt Sallies'. Others told fortunes or ran boxing booths where young bucks were invited to step up and fight for a purse that they seldom won. From those booths came many a champion bare-knuckle fighter of Gypsy origin.

Not all Gypsies were horse dealers, however, and not all horse dealers earned enough from their trade to keep their families fed and clothed throughout the year. Wherever in Britain they were, in rural areas work was to be found mending fences, digging ditches or laying hedges. In springtime, in the hop-growing parishes of Herefordshire, Worcestershire, Hampshire, Sussex and Kent, hands were required to tie hops to their supports. In the summer months there were soft fruits to be picked and later in the year, during September and October, the hops and apples to be brought in.

For Scottish Travellers, in addition to the usual agricultural work, there were opportunities to earn money in the summertime from pearl fishing in the rivers Tay, Spey, Dee and Esk, amongst others. In July there were raspberries to be harvested. Larch-peeling, for the dye, was available from April, the season lasting a few weeks, and beaters were required on the big estates during the shooting season.

Opposite:
Matthew Wood,
a knife-grinder,
also advertised
the 'careful
mending of
china and glass'.

Above: Horses have always been an important part of Gypsy life. A good horse was necessary for pulling a wagon, and dealing in horses brought in much-needed income.

Some farmers flatly refused to employ Gypsies but others recognised the benefits of doing so, one of which was that there was no need to provide a roof over their heads. They also arrived when labour was required and left when the harvest was finished.

In periods when the demand for casual labour fell, time was spent making items that could then be sold. Peg-making, as with any other rural craft, was passed on from father to son for generations, and whole families could be involved in the making of pegs, with the smallest children gathering up the shavings to burn on the fire. The preferred wood was willow, and

Above middle: An encampment of hoppers in Kent in 1904. Hop growers welcomed Gypsies for the harvest because they had no need to provide accommodation for them.

Right: A family hop-picking at Yalding, Kent. During September and October hundreds of Gypsies made the annual trip to the hop gardens.

the metal used for the tinning came from old cans and containers. The only tools required were a pair of pincers, a very sharp knife, and a hammer for knocking in the nail that held the tin strip to the peg.

As many as four dozen pegs could be made in an hour. According to an old Gypsy man speaking on a BBC Home Service radio broadcast in 1940,

Above: Peg-making was a craft passed down the generations.

That's the or'nary size pegs; we make different sizes, you know. Little uns for the light washing like hankichers an' ladies' thingummyjigs, an' big great heavy uns for blankets, but biggest sale is for the middlin' size.

Left: The travelling basket-maker's living wagon also served as his shop. His wares were carried on the top and hung from the sides of the wagon.

Sharp peg knives could also be turned to making wooden flowers, which were coloured with natural dyes made from berries and foliage, and then sold to housewives, or at back doors to servant girls.

A wide variety of items were manufactured. Customers for hand-made baskets included bakers, fruiterers, fishermen and householders who required them for coal, wood or laundry. Butchers needed skewers, and housewives required brooms to sweep their floors. Other items that were made from freely available materials included bee-skeps, rush whips, mats, carpet-beaters and even dolls' house furniture. Spoons made from bone were a particular talent of Scottish Travellers.

It was mainly the women who went from door to door hawking the hand-made products and smaller, bought-in items such as lace and ribbons. Larger goods, including carpets

Britannia Orchard, a broom hawker. Brooms were sometimes hand-made, but others were bought in from wholesalers.

and curtains bought from factories in the Midlands, were taken around by horse and cart. One annual visitor to Brighton arrived with not just curtains but also clothes that she had been given from the back doors of the big houses at which she had called en route to the town. Her regular customers eagerly

A bee-skep maker. In some cases, the straw used in the making of the skeps was passed through a ram's horn to hold it tight.

A typical hawking basket, or 'kipsie', appears to hold groceries, an indication that these women are returning from a successful day's hawking.

anticipated her arrival and could expect to be given first pick of the finery on offer.

Skills extended to chair mending, tinkering, and china riveting. The knife-grinder was a welcome return visitor to both rural and urban areas. Two hundred years ago, his machine may well have been home-made, perhaps pushed around on a handcart or carried on a donkey, or possibly on his back. He either went from door to door offering his services or set up on market day in the village square, where customers would bring their blunt knives for him to sharpen. Similarly, the *mush-fakir* – or umbrella mender – and chair bottomer set up where they could be easily seen.

Francie Marshall clipping a sheet of horn. Spoons made from horn were a speciality of Border Gypsies and Scottish Travellers. From *The Tinkler-Gypsies of Galloway* by Andrew McCormick, 1906.

In towns there was different employment to be found. There was an income to be made from dealing in rags and bones or in second-hand furniture. Other Gypsies worked as ostlers or cellarmen, or found work that afforded them a degree of independence, such as fly-driving or coal heaving. Women continued with the hawking but occasionally the men sold fruit, vegetables or fish from barrows.

For those who had been taught the art of character reading from a very young age, going out calling with the hawking basket opened the doors to a spot of opportunistic

'dukkering', or fortune-telling. A few additional coins could be obtained from housewives on their front doorsteps or from the servant girls at tradesmen's entrances of larger houses. Their employers sought to have their fortunes read by the Gypsies who frequented pleasure gardens.

Gypsy fortune-tellers could be found in the south London area from at least the seventeenth century. Samuel Pepys noted in his diary for 11 August 1688 that his wife had visited the Gypsies at Lambeth to have her fortune told. An attraction at Norwood was the fortune-telling of Margaret Finch, so-called 'Queen of the Gypsies', who died in 1740, and her fame drew vast crowds of all classes. As Prince of Wales, King George III was also a visitor to the Gypsies of Norwood and, when they moved to a neighbouring wood in Dulwich, they were constantly visited by Lord Byron when he played truant from his school.

A knife-grinding barrow that was used by John Smith, a Gypsy, until 1966 is exhibited at Worcestershire County Museum at Hartlebury Castle.

Fortune-tellers frequented pleasure gardens throughout the country. Their customers came from all walks of life. From an original print.

Not all Gypsies have second sight, but some undoubtedly do. In 1897 Urania Boswell predicted that 'Queen Victoria would see the leaves fall four times before her long rest', and, at Henley Regatta, warned a Mr Vanderbilt against sailing on the *Titanic* on its maiden voyage – advice which saved his life. She foresaw her own son's death and that of her brother, and, on the Saturday before she herself died, correctly predicted that 'On the third day from now I shall die and on that day it will rain'.

The progression to the seaside from the pleasure gardens where the Gypsy fortune -tellers plied their trade, often dressed for the part in fringed shawls and elaborate headdresses, was inevitable. The growth in the leisure industry during the latter half of the nineteenth century attracted increasing numbers of visitors to coastal towns. Gypsy fortune-tellers followed and set up booths. In addition, family members took the opportunity to offer donkey and pony rides on the sands or set up their coconut shies and sideshows. In some resorts, work was also found in the developing fairgrounds.

On the South Shore, Blackpool, a colony of Gypsies set up home on the sand and their encampment became a popular tourist attraction in its own right, so much so that a miniature railway track ran around the perimeter and incorporated a stop at Gypsyville Station.

A successful entrepreneur at the seaside could make enough money in the summer to last him throughout the winter months, but a regular

Donkey proprietors on Hampstead Heath. Gypsies and others offered donkey and pony rides in many parks. *Illustrated London News,* October 1875.

33

income could not be guaranteed when travelling, and a scarcity of work often resulted in real poverty and hardship. There were only so many chairs and umbrellas to be mended and knives to sharpen but, for those who had the knowledge and experience, there were other services to fall back on, such as chimney sweeping or vermin extermination. Low-paid cottage dwellers had their own ways of cleaning their chimneys, but a large country house with many rooms heated by open fires was a bonus to the travelling sweep, and, no matter how grand the house or lowly the barn, rats were a recurring problem for farmers, tradespeople and gentry alike. If the mill-owner needed rats to be dispatched from his store, so did the highest of the land from their palaces.

Reuben Herron and his wife on Epsom Downs in May 1937.

In 1836 the then Princess Victoria met some Gypsies who were camping opposite the gates of Claremont House in Esher, Surrey. During their stay she came to know them well. Among them was a young couple waiting for the imminent birth of their first child, and the Princess had clothes sent out for the baby. Some years later the father, Matthias (Matty) Cooper, was employed to catch rats at Hampton Court Palace and Windsor Castle. Whether he exploited his earlier brief acquaintance with the Queen to obtain work is unknown, but family legend has it that, when he died in 1901, Queen Victoria had a wreath of yellow flowers placed upon his grave. He is often referred to as the 'Royal Rat Catcher'.

Mattie Cooper, the 'Royal Rat Catcher', was a well-known visitor to race meetings and other events in southern England.

His grandson Vanselo, many years after Matty's death, claimed that his grandfather had caught as many as two bushels of rats at Windsor Castle and laid them out on the carpet in front of Queen Victoria. Edward, Prince of Wales, was so impressed that he gave Matty half a sovereign. Matty Cooper's secret as a successful rat-catcher, according to Vanselo, was the quantity of yew leaves he added to the preparation when he was boiling it up.

During Victoria's reign Gypsies came into contact with members of the Royal Family fairly frequently. The Prince of Wales was in the habit of throwing coins to the Gypsy children at race meetings and Vanselo Cooper recalled receiving many half-crowns from him at Ascot races.

In 1889 John Roberts, a renowned Welsh Gypsy harpist, and his nine sons gave a performance for Queen Victoria in Bala, North Wales. Between them his sons played pedal harp, Welsh harp, English harp, triple harp, violin, double bass violin, flageolet and piccolo. He had enlisted in the Royal Welsh Fusiliers as a drummer boy when he was aged fourteen and was taught to read music. He deserted twice, although he was credited with having served nine years, and eventually managed to buy himself out in 1844 with the money he earned as a harpist, two years after winning the harp prize at the Eisteddfod in Abergavenny.

Oliver Lee with his fiddle at Llangollen in May 1913.

The Wood family of Wales was closely connected to the Roberts family. They too were proficient on the fiddle and harp and, like so many other Gypsy families, numbered good step and clog dancers among them.

In Scotland, Traveller pipe players were occasionally employed to play at the big houses. The MacPhees were considered the main clan of itinerant pipers, the art being passed from father to son, while in the Borders James Allan, born in Northumberland in 1734, was in equal measures a renowned thief and a player of the Northumbrian pipes of considerable talent. He was taught to play by his father and carried the old tunes from village to village. His reputation as a player of the pipes led to him being appointed the Countess of Northumberland's personal piper, a post he remained in for two years, after which he became Regimental Piper in the Northumberland Militia. In the Lowlands, on the Borders and in the north of England, the Northumbrian pipes were once recognised to be a Gypsy instrument.

In the early nineteenth century Gypsy entertainers included bear-leaders, acrobats, dancers and harp players, but it was the fiddle players who were in particular demand. In the eighteenth century a celebration called the Marsh Bush was held on Whit Sunday at Headington near Oxford, which, according to the memories of the elderly in 1804, was attended by Gypsy fiddlers. Writing in the *Journal of the Gypsy Lore Society* in 1908, Lucy Broadwood recalled hearing from a Northamptonshire woman many years previously that the local farmer used to hire local Gypsy musicians to play and sing for them at their dances and gatherings.

Even those without musical accomplishment found ways to entertain the host society. In the 1850s Ambrose Smith and his people, the so-called Epping Forest Gypsies, spent much of the year touring Britain, hiring assembly rooms and halls at which they organised grand balls, one of which purportedly attracted two thousand people at sixpence a time admission fee. If Gypsy musicians were unavailable, they simply hired from the local community. When travelling with them, Gypsy musicians dressed for the occasion in long black coats, brightly coloured waistcoats, velvet knee-breeches and smart top-boots. Thus attired, they fiddled for the dancing from early morning until dark, while the women collected the money in tambourines.

From the late nineteenth century onwards leisure time for low-paid workers was minimal and entertainment was largely home-based. Those lucky enough to own a piano gathered people around it and sang the popular songs of the day. Similarly, travelling folk, returning from a day's work or from an evening in the pub, sat around the camp fire and sang the songs their forefathers had picked up as they passed from village to village. In 1907 Cecil Sharpe, a folk-song collector who founded the English Folk Dance Society in 1911, was astonished to be treated to 'the first and most characterful bit of singing I have ever heard' by Betsy Holland, a Gypsy woman he met by chance in Devon. Betsy had learned her song from her grandmother.

At about the same time, Alice Gillington, a woman who had taken to living in a caravan in Hampshire,

Scottish Traveller William Marshall performing an impromptu dance. From *The Tinkler-Gypsies of Galloway* by Andrew McCormick, 1906.

was collecting songs and stories from the Gypsies who frequented the New Forest. From the 1960s through to the 1970s, a new generation of collectors began visiting Gypsies and Scottish Travellers in their houses and encampments to record on tape the songs that continued to be passed down. While the old songs had become lost to the settled population, they were retained by the travelling folk because of their relative isolation from outsiders

As well as being the keepers of the old songs and music, Gypsies and Travellers were great story-tellers and proved to be a rich source of folk tales for the folklorists of the late Victorian and Edwardian era.

Story-teller
Mary MacMillan,
a Scottish Traveller,
was reputed to be
able to spin a
story out for
hours. From
*The Tinkler-Gypsies
of Galloway*
by Andrew
McCormick, 1906.

EVANGELISM AND
WAR WORK

IN THE EIGHTEENTH CENTURY the church, both traditional and nonconformist, began to turn its thoughts to the 'heathen' Gypsies. Concern was voiced about their vagabond lifestyle and lack of education. With education and 'soul saving' it was hoped the wanderers could be persuaded to turn their backs on their traditions and the perceived evils of fortune-telling. Evangelical work amongst the Gypsies flourished from the mid-nineteenth century, although a few young Gypsies attended some form of Sunday school in the early years of the century.

At that time it was often the Sunday schools that provided basic reading and writing skills to the poor. In London in 1811, Thomas Howard, owner of a glass and china shop just off Fleet Street, and part-time Calvinist preacher, helped to establish a Sunday school near Clapham, principally for the neglected children of local brick-makers. The thirteen-year-old girl from a family that had taken winter lodgings opposite made regular attempts

Evangelism was widespread in the nineteenth and early twentieth centuries. Mission wagons, such as this one, were regularly seen at fairs and during the hop and fruit harvests.

At hop-picking time missionaries encouraged Gypsies to have their children baptised. Often three or four babies were baptised on the same day.

to attend but each time was refused because she was a Gypsy. But her persistence paid off and she and her two brothers were eventually allowed admission. Following this, a number of Gypsy children were admitted to a Sunday school run by Stockwell Chapel, and also to one at Norwood, where many travelling Gypsies arrived each year to overwinter. Others were sent to St Patrick's charity school, although a number were later moved to the nearby school for the Irish because of concern over the religion of the former.

Classes at Sunday schools were mainly concerned with teaching children to read the scriptures, but by the 1830s missionaries and clergymen were visiting Epsom racecourse and the hop-picking parishes of Hampshire, Surrey and beyond to preach to the adults. The Reverend James Crabb recruited a Gypsy preacher, William Stanley, to help him spread the gospel, sending him ahead to pave the way for the reforming missionaries. As a youth, Stanley had signed up to the Wiltshire Militia and while stationed at Exeter had been invited to attend a service at a Wesleyan chapel, during which he became a convert. Later, in 1844, he laid the foundation stone of the short-lived Farnham Gipsy School and Asylum in Dorset.

In Scotland, at Kirk Yetholm, encouraged by James Crabb's efforts, the Reverend John Baird thought that, by directing his attention to the Gypsy children there, he would eventually persuade the parents to give up the vagabond life. His plan was to prevent the children from travelling,

Rodney 'Gypsy' Smith travelled three times around the world preaching.

send them to school, and lodge them with local families while their parents were away, in the belief that separation from their children would persuade the adults to take up permanent residence. His efforts were met with only partial success.

The London City Mission fared a little better. By the 1850s its missionaries were visiting encampments around the city and also holding regular social events in local halls. Children were found places in day, evening and missionary schools in the Notting Hill district and the Kensington potteries. Towards the end of the century the 'Gipsies' Hall', a mission for Battersea van-dwellers, was set up in a railway arch and was well attended, with a few giving up fortune-telling and some becoming evangelists themselves. Following a more formal route, on returning to Britain after many years spent in the United States, one wealthy Gypsy sent his son to theological college, intent on him becoming a nonconformist minister, which he did, eventually accepting the living of a church in Yorkshire.

Although there were a number of Gypsies spreading the gospel in the later nineteenth century, including a few women, it was Rodney Smith, born into the travelling life in 1860, who eventually became the most famous of Gypsy preachers. He and his parents traversed the country by wagon, earning a living by selling baskets and clothes pegs. His father, Cornelius, occasionally earned money by playing the fiddle in pubs, where Rodney provided additional entertainment by dancing to his father's tunes.

Cornelius was born in a tent in Burwell, Cambridgeshire, in 1831, to parents who were chair-caners and basket-makers. As an adult, he became much in demand as a fiddle-player, a pastime that was considered by some to be the work of the devil. After reading a borrowed copy of John Bunyan's *A Pilgrim's Progress*, he and his brother Bartholomew set out on the road to become preachers. They held their first prayer meeting in a Gypsy tent and very soon afterwards were joined by their brother Woodlock. Cornelius dispensed with his fiddle at a pawnshop but was later to meet William Booth, who encouraged him to acquire a new one to use in his missionary work. Collectively, the brothers became known as 'the three converted Gypsies', working as a team to spread the gospel.

Some years later, Bartholomew's son Simon became a missionary in the slums of London. Born in a wagon in Epping Forest, he was just eleven years old when he presented himself at the door of Thomas Barnardo and asked to be sent to Canada to work, in order to send money home to his widowed mother. He worked on a farm for two years before returning to England. It was while employed as a cab driver in London that he by chance heard a woman singing a hymn and became an immediate convert, after which he went to work for the London City Mission. Known as 'the silvery voiced tenor from the woods', as an evangelist he travelled far and wide and, though less well-known than his cousin Rodney, he nonetheless spent forty years in missionary work on both sides of the Atlantic, eventually moving his family to Canada and settling in London, Ontario.

Rodney Smith had no formal education and, after becoming a Christian, taught himself to read and write with the aid of a Bible, a Bible dictionary and an English dictionary. Aged seventeen, at the invitation of William Booth, he became an evangelist for the Christian Mission of London, later to become the Salvation Army. He preached on street corners and in mission halls for six years. In the early 1880s he conducted a great mission at Hanley. There two Gypsy sisters, Trypheni and Miriam Boswell, met the Salvation Army officers who were to become their husbands. Trypheni joined a small band of Gypsy women already taking the gospel out to the people. Soon afterwards she became a missionary overseas.

Rodney Smith's first trip abroad, to Sweden, was in 1893 and he later visited the United States and Australia, the former at least thirty times, and twice he preached his way around the world. He was a charismatic figure and could fill a venue to overflowing. After a particularly good series of meetings in Edinburgh in 1892, the Gypsy Gospel Wagon Mission was formed to take the gospel out to the Gypsies.

Cornelius had set a path for subsequent generations to follow. Rodney's son, Albany, served as an evangelist in the United States from 1911 until 1951, and another of his sons, Alfred, was a Wesleyan pastor in England. Albany's son became a Presbyterian pastor. Rodney's younger sister, Matilda, was the mother of George Bramwell Evans, a Methodist minister who became well-known as 'Romany of the BBC'. He was radio's first wildlife presenter, his 'Out with Romany' series being broadcast on *Children's Hour* from 1932 until his death in 1942. The family tradition has continued into the twenty-first century. George Bramwell Evans's grandson, Roly Bain, was ordained in the Church of England and in 1982 helped to found 'Holy Fool', a network of Christians committed to clowning in ministry and worship.

In the First World War, too old to enlist, Rodney Smith travelled to the battlefields of France to minister to the British troops, often on the front line. He distributed items such as soap, candles and buttons, and served tea and coffee to young soldiers who were often trembling with fever or shell-shock.

George Bramwell Evans, well-known as 'Romany of the BBC', was the nephew of Rodney Smith.

41

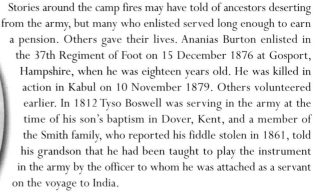

Stories around the camp fires may have told of ancestors deserting from the army, but many who enlisted served long enough to earn a pension. Others gave their lives. Ananias Burton enlisted in the 37th Regiment of Foot on 15 December 1876 at Gosport, Hampshire, when he was eighteen years old. He was killed in action in Kabul on 10 November 1879. Others volunteered earlier. In 1812 Tyso Boswell was serving in the army at the time of his son's baptism in Dover, Kent, and a member of the Smith family, who reported his fiddle stolen in 1861, told his grandson that he had been taught to play the instrument in the army by the officer to whom he was attached as a servant on the voyage to India.

Guardsman Edward Hope, a Gypsy.

Gypsies and Travellers were not exempt from military service in either of the two world wars. Those following the travelling life did not keep regular hours but they did often work long days, traipsing around in their search for scrap or rags, or customers for their services. Call-up could be difficult with such mobile people; moreover, many Gypsies were unable to read and so could not follow the orders from the recruiting posters or newspapers that called them to arms. Those in charge of recruitment, therefore, had to make a special effort to search out the travelling folk, not always an easy task if the encampment was hidden away in a sheltered spot.

Some families have stories of mothers allegedly disguising their sons as daughters to avoid military service, a desperate action that was not unknown amongst the settled community also, but many did not wait for the call-up.

Thomas Orchard with his wife, Britannia. There were Gypsy soldiers in most regiments during the First World War.

Family tradition recounts that when a Gypsy soldier who served in both the Boer War and the First World War was invalided out of the army on a small pension, his father-in-law used traditional horse remedies to treat his wounded leg. Unfortunately, when it healed, the pension stopped. Though the father-in-law's equine knowledge, having had both positive and negative results, may not have been fully appreciated by the patient, when war broke out in 1914 many of those Gypsies who presented themselves at the recruiting office found their long association and expertise with horses was fully recognised, and consequently they were sent into the Veterinary Corps. Silvester Gordon Boswell joined up in 1915 and was sent to Woolwich Common for training. He passed out as First Class Veterinary Dresser and was sent to a veterinary hospital about 3 km from Boulogne. Six of his brothers also fought in France.

The sacrifice made by families from all sections of society was often huge, including those from the travelling tradition. Silvester Boswell's family was not alone in sending all its sons off to war. A branch of the Penfold family waved off five sons, the Hughes family lost three of the five sons who served in the Duke of Cornwall's Light Infantry, and the Scamp family of Kent lost at least two of their sons.

John Cole was another Gypsy to serve in the First World War.

Barbara Walsh, a Surrey-based Romany, recounted her late mother's poignant memories of her uncle Abraham Ripley and his nephew and best friend, also Abraham, marching away from the family together:

> Everyone went out of the yard to see them off. The two young Abrahams laughed as they waved and walked away into their uncertain future. The family stood in silence until the two had disappeared, then they went back to the yard until only my mother stood looking down the empty lane, even after the sound of their boots and their laughter had died away. The name Abraham Ripley is recorded twice on the memorial at Hailsham, Sussex, and their young lives were just two amongst the millions that were lost in that dreadful conflict.

The talents of the Gypsies could be used to the military's advantage, a good example being Silvester Boswell's placement in the Veterinary Corps. Retraining took time and money. Poaching rabbits and small game was a not uncommon pursuit in the countryside, and not just by Gypsies. It required certain skills: stealth, the ability to remain motionless for long periods at

Right: William Webb was in the Air Force Volunteer Reserve, serving with Headquarters 3rd Tactical Air Force based in Camilla, India, when he died on 11 December 1944, aged twenty-two.

Below: At the outbreak of war Ron Gray lied about his age and signed up in the 45th Royal Marine Commandos. He fought in Germany, Burma and Ceylon.

Right: Henry Keet served three years in India before the outbreak of the Second World War. War service took him to North Africa and Europe.

Far right: Land Army girls Blanche and Nell Smith, the daughters of William Smith and Milly Doe.

a time, a steady hand on the shotgun, and good night-time vision. In short, the poacher made the perfect sniper. In enemy territory, he was also an asset when it came to foraging for food.

In the Second World War sixty per cent of the records of soldiers who served in the First World War were destroyed by enemy bombing, but amongst the forty per cent remaining many Gypsy names are to be found.

The Medal Rolls are further evidence of Gypsy and Traveller participation. In addition to the campaign medals awarded, there are a number of Military Medals and at least one Victoria Cross; Jack Cunningham was born in 1897 to licensed hawkers who traded in oilcloth and carpets. He volunteered, aged seventeen, for the East Yorkshire Regiment and was sent to the Somme. When the rest of his bombing party were either killed or injured during the Battle of Ancre on 13 November 1916, he continued alone, taking their bombs to attack the German trenches. When he had used them all, he collected fresh supplies and returned for a second attack, clearing the trench up to the enemy line.

When the menfolk were away fighting, women on the home front left their wagons and tents to work in munitions factories or on the land.

In the Second World War some served with the Auxiliary Territorial Service (ATS) or the Land Army, others drove ambulances, became auxiliary nurses, or served as Air Raid Precautions (ARP) wardens. One young woman who joined the Women's Royal Naval Service (WRNS) served in Signals Intelligence at Bletchley Park and its outstations, intercepting messages transmitted from German naval bases to their ships at sea.

Men who were unfit for active service were recruited to use their skills in the civilian war effort. Experienced net-makers turned their hands to making camouflage nets from rope, and cargo nets and slings. Others used their skills as menders of pots and pans to solder containers and storage batteries. In the forests, men felled trees to convert into industrial timbers. Women also worked in tree nurseries. In the New Forest Gypsies were employed in the gathering of acorns for feeding pigs, and of alder buckthorn, which was used in making high-grade charcoal. This in turn was used in the manufacture of best-quality black gunpowder. In the cities, gangs of demolition workers cleared up after the Blitz.

When peace came, most men and women returned to their traditional occupations and way of life, but war had forced many into close contact with the settled community and into regular, waged work, at least for the duration of hostilities. Of those, some made the choice to settle permanently.

Left: During the War Nancy Millis served in Signals Intelligence at Bletchley Park and continued in the Women's Royal Naval Reserve until 1953.

Below left: A Gypsy woman making a net for catching rabbits. During the Second World War Gypsies were employed in making camouflage nets.

Below: Wearing a WAAF uniform to commemorate fifty years of the women's services, this Romany airwoman took part in the 1968 Festival of Remembrance at the Royal Albert Hall.

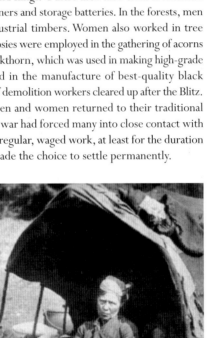

THE TWENTY-FIRST CENTURY

OVER THE YEARS Gypsies have had to adapt to the changing times. Although some travel throughout the spring and summer, for a variety of reasons the majority now live in houses. Travelling is by modern trailer, rather than the painted wagon of yesteryear. If groups of horse-drawn wagons do appear on roadside verges, they are more often than not occupied by New Travellers.

Traditional stopping places have disappeared under tarmac or have been built upon, and industrial estates have sprung up on the periphery of towns where once the travelling folk pulled up for the winter. For those stopping places that still exist, there is competition from other, much larger groups of Travellers who need to break their journey. There is stiff competition, too, for the permanent sites among those who want to give up the travelling life but wish to remain amongst those who share their culture. Those who stop on the verges face the constant threat of being moved on.

Work opportunities have also diminished. Farming methods have changed dramatically since the early half of the twentieth century. There has been a sharp decline in the trade of horses, so few of the old horse fairs remain. Even so, the pilgrimage to Appleby-in-Westmorland and Stow-on-the-Wold each year to show off their horses and to set up market stalls continues, and smaller fairs such as Wickham in Hampshire are popular with local families.

The cutting back and laying of hedges would once have guaranteed a few days' work, but fewer hedges are managed in the traditional way now, and one man and a tractor can cut back a farm's boundary in a fraction of the time it would have taken a small team of men.

The small acreage of hops that remains is, like apples and pears, mainly grown on dwarf stock and largely harvested by machine. One or two families may make their way to the cherry orchards and strawberry fields each year, more out of a sense of nostalgia than by necessity, but the harvesting of the soft-fruit crop attracts mainly students and workers from overseas.

Demand for hand-crafted baskets and pegs plummeted with the import of cheap, factory-made products, but these skills have not disappeared altogether; there is still an outlet for them among the non-Gypsy visitors to

Opposite:
Ambrose Cooper,
a Gypsy singer,
on the steps of a
bow-top wagon.

47

A trader at
a horse fair.

places such as Appleby. Raw materials continue to be gathered, but often under contract to landowners, and are sold on to florists and wholesale markets such as Covent Garden.

And so the occupations have changed to suit the modern age. The sons and daughters of the travelling hawkers have become market stallholders, horse traders have become car mechanics, and the rag and bone men have moved into recycling, with some owning large paper mills. Others are demolition or building contractors. Hedging and ditching have been replaced by landscape

A good horse is
a valuable asset;
traders at a horse
fair in Norfolk.

gardening. Some may continue to learn their skills from their fathers, but others attend college to gain both practical experience and formal qualifications. It is no longer unusual to find Gypsies with diplomas, university degrees

or doctorates because settlement has enabled education, for those who are able to access it, to be continued into adulthood, rather than curtailed each time of moving on. Therefore, well-qualified individuals of Gypsy and Traveller heritage are to be found as teachers, university tutors, nurses, journalists and social workers. In the art world, there are professional actors, choreographers, musicians, authors and artists.

Professor Ian Hancock (right), one of many British Gypsies to have achieved distinction in the academic world.

A line of bow-top wagons at a Gypsy festival in Sussex.

Romani Rad, a group of eastern European Roma musicians now living in England. Since the European Union has expanded, Romanies are once again travelling over from the mainland.

Traders at a horse fair in Norfolk.

Gypsies continue to serve in the armed forces, their tours of duty taking them to the world's trouble spots, and others represent the country in the boxing ring, a natural progression, perhaps, from the pugilism of their ancestors, and accomplished horsemen and women compete in various events at world-class level.

Settlement, however, and the downturn in seasonal work have left fewer opportunities for extended families and friends to gather together. This gap, in some way, has been filled by the Pentecostal movement that started amongst the Roma in Europe in the 1950s and has since swept through Britain's Gypsy communities. Formerly it was predominantly non-Gypsy ministers who arrived in the hop gardens and fruit fields with their mission tents, but now the Gypsy-led Light and Life Church and Gypsies for Christ hold conventions under canvas that attract hundreds of converts each year. Their churches are spread throughout Britain.

Well-maintained horse-drawn vehicles at a Gypsy festival.

Music and song are still very much part of Gypsy culture. This talented Gypsy girl has been singing since she was small.

Times may have changed, but tradition and culture continue to play a part in both settled and travelling life. Great pride is taken in the ownership and exhibiting of traditional wagons and other horse-drawn vehicles, even if they are more likely to be transported to events by low-loader than pulled by horse.

Music and song are seldom far away. Country music tends to be the popular choice and, in such a close community, when meeting together, both children and adults need little encouragement to sing. Gypsy children have performed in musicals at London theatres, and the Romany Theatre Company, founded in 2002, and the Romani Cultural and Arts Company, founded in Wales in 2009, have both showcased the talents of young Gypsies and Travellers.

Gypsy story-tellers take their craft into schools and folk clubs, and musicians and singers are in demand at festivals.

Gypsy story-teller Richard O'Neil follows an age-old tradition. He is also a motivational speaker.

The stereotypical image of Gypsies may continue to be that of a mysterious, swarthy people travelling around in brightly painted horse-drawn wagons, but this has always been an over-romanticised idyll. Living wagons could be seen around the lanes as late as the 1970s, but some families dispensed with them as early as the 1920s and adopted caravans pulled by lorries. Over the centuries, marriages with non-Gypsies may have taken place, but cultural ties and traditions have remained strong and, as with any other segment of society, Gypsies have had to adapt to the changing times.

Travelling, by wagon or trailer, is not an easy option in the modern world. While Gypsies were once a recognised, if sometimes barely tolerated, part of British life, appearing as they did for the harvest when required, or bringing wares and skills to towns and rural areas, their services are no longer required. A travelling life is not easy to relinquish for a people who have been seasonally nomadic for centuries, but there is increasing pressure on them to become settled. In 1811 John Hoyland, a Quaker, wrote of his concerns that Gypsies were constantly being moved on without anywhere being provided for them to go. In a country where so many changes have been made over the past two centuries, some things seemed destined to remain the same.

Jess Smith, a Scottish Traveller, with her husband. Jess is a story-teller, singer and author.

A young man puts his horse through its paces.

PLACES TO VISIT

Gordon Boswell Romany Museum, Clay Lake, Spalding, Lincolnshire PE12 6BL.
Telephone: 01775 710599. Website: www.boswell-romany-museum.com
Museum of East Anglian Life, Crowe Street, Stowmarket, Suffolk IP14 1DL.
Telephone: 01449 612 229. Website: eastanglianlife.org.uk
Ryedale Folk Museum, Hutton le Hole, North Yorkshire YO62 6UA.
Telephone: 01751 417 367. Website: www.ryedalefolkmuseum.co.uk
Worcestershire County Museum, Hartlebury Castle, Hartlebury Nr
Kidderminster, Worcestershire DY11 7XZ. Telephone: 01299 250416.
Website: www.whub.org.uk/cms/museums-
worcestershire/hartlebury.aspx
South East Romany Museum, Twin Oaks, Howland Road, Marden, Kent,
TN12 9LB. Telephone: 07964 373963.
Website: www.southeastromanymuseum.co.uk

Wagons and
dealing – a
good day out.

FURTHER READING

Crabb, Rev. James. *The Gipsies' Advocate* [1832]. Romany & Traveller Family
  History Society, 2007.

Dawson, Robert. *Empty Lands: Aspects of Scottish Traveller Survival.*
  Robert Dawson, 2007.

Fraser, Angus. *The Gypsies*. Blackwell, 1995.

Hoyland, John. *The Gypsies* [1816]. Romany & Traveller Family
  History Society, 2004.

Jarman, A. O. H. and Eldra. *The Welsh Gypsies: Children of Abram Wood*,
  UOW Press, 1991.

Mayall, David. *Gypsy-Travellers in Nineteenth-century Society*. Cambridge
  University Press, 2009.

Smith, Len. Romany *Nevi-Wesh: an Informal History of the New Forest Gypsies.*
  Nova Foresta Publishing, 2004.

INDEX